Chalky Boulders

Linda West

First published in 2022 by Paragon Publishing, Rothersthorpe

ISBN 978-1-78222-929-2

Book design, layout and production management by Into Print
www.intoprint.net
+44 (0)1604 832149

Dedication

I would like to dedicate this book
To the dear friends and family
Who take the time to have a look

Also, a special thank you to my husband Chris who patiently listens to my poems morning, noon or night.

CONTENTS

Free

Cast your nets wide, flow and ebb with the tide
Give yourself up to the vastness of the sea
Dance with white horses, be yourself...
Free!

FOREWORD

The Birth of 'Chalky Boulders'

Hello, thank you for taking the time to read my second book *Chalky Boulders*.

My second book, the first one being *Membrane Towers*, is an eclectic mix of new poetry which hopefully will appeal to all of your emotions and give yourself some idea of who I am as both a person, and as someone who writes down collections of words, some rhyming, some not, which appear, without warning in my head and compel me to commit them to paper. I have never considered myself to be a poet!

The reason I have chosen to write this second book is quite simple: as with the first book, I wanted to leave something of myself behind for my present and future family and a book is a perfect opportunity. I never knew my own grandparents; they were all deceased by the time I was old enough to understand who they were and consequently, they remain just names on a family tree. I really wish they had left something for me to connect to; there is nothing, just a couple of faded old photos and this I have always considered to be sad.

Through publishing my books I am leaving behind, a lifetime of writing rhyme for family and friends, a personal testimony which hopefully celebrates a small part of who I am, who I was, who I have become, and who I hope to become, something tangible, something to hold and connect to.

I hope the poems speak to you in the way they have spoken to me.

Love Lin x

Alternative Humour

BACK IN THE DAYS

I'm taking a few moments to wander back in time
Why not come with me, be my partner in crime
See yourself in the mirror, that taut unwrinkled skin,
The smoothness, the contour, no hairs on your chin!

Remember those miniskirts, short and oh so tight
High heels, blistered feet, from dancing all night!
Flower power; ban the bomb, the swinging sixties
Hair styles, The Beehive, The Bobs and the Pixies

Such wonderful times, so vivid within my head
Listening to Luxembourg on my transistor in bed
Watching the wrestling on a Saturday afternoon
In between the football results, over far too soon

All ingrained in my brain, often remembered and said
The 1966 world cup team, most of them now dead
Turning on the black and white telly, ages to warm up
Time to boil the cabbage to death, make a cuppa to sup!

The Palladium, The Avengers, The Saint and Dad's Army
Not forgetting The Flintstones with funny old Fred and Barny
What about Crackerjack, with dear Lesley, double or drop.
Blue Peter, with guest Lulu, the naughty elephant who plopped!

Remember the famous Cavern, Paul, Ringo George and John
The fab four Beatles, although now George and John long gone
This Boy, Michelle, Yesterday and so many, many more
Smooching with the boy of the night, on the dance hall floor

What about playing Hop Scotch, Chucks and Skipping
in the road
No traffic to speak of and certainly no streets paved with gold
Two ball and kick the can, knocky –eye–doe, finger or thumb
Games played in the street; we made our own kind of fun

Jam and sugar sandwiches, beef dripping and lemon curd
Could never have an opinion, children seen and not heard
No Chinese, no, KFC or McDonald's salt to do us harm
The only McDonalds I knew was the one who had a farm

With a moo moo here and a bar bar there, oh, yes
we loved our drink
Gin and orange, Gin and lime, Gin and everything, not yet pink
The pubs were always packed, on a Friday, Saturday night
Bingo, Bat and Trap, drunks a plenty and the predictable fight

Off we'd scarper, not to be found, we were not easy to track
No internet, no Instagram and most of all nosey Apps
I don't envy today's youth, like you, I am a child of my time
Less pressure back in the days, no mobile phone, less crime

But then where I grew up no one had anything to pinch
Doors were left wide open, getting in always a cinch
Particularly when playing truant, not going back to school
I'd cover my shoes in dirt and rubble, my mum was no fool

I was brought up to be honest, and always tell the truth
Always sit tidy, no swearing, it's considered uncouth
And yet no one liked us despite our kind loyal ways
We were considered to be common, dirty, back in the days,

But I never feared my safety, when outside, not at all
For a bond like elastic stretched around us should we fall
But I don't fall down very often; I am made of stern stuff
My Mam and Dad brought me up to be stoic, never rough

Oh yes, my parents were strict, I had a few clouts in my time
Through getting into trouble, with those teenage friends of mine
But, I'm grateful to Mum for protection, Polio, Small Pox,
and TB
But I am more grateful that back in the days
they did not have CCTV!

BLIND DATE

He hurries along, the lyrics of a song,
Softly soothe the panic in his head.
Watching and waiting, anticipating
To appease this feeling of dread!

What will he say, how will he start
It's been such a very long time,
He practises his smile, he waits to beguile
The stranger, he met when online!

His heart is as heavy as the lump in his throat,
His patience, like his time, comes and goes
The song is sung, he goes home to his Mum,
He's wasted the price of a rose!

BLOGGERLESS

I've sat here for a lifetime my whole brain is numb
I don't know how to do it; I don't know how it's done
I want to have my own blog, like TMZ and The Verge
I'm hoping for a boost, a huge confidence surge!
I'm aiming to promote my poems, gain internet fame
Just placing a few on Facebook is really not the same!
I have trawled through YouTube, struggled to no avail
I going to be really honest; I can't make head nor tail
I want to be as renowned as The Huffington Post
People watching my blog as they eat their toast
But something does tell me, after an Eon of trying
Me and my Blog plan, like my battery, is quickly dying
So I might need to admit, I may never be a blogger
On the other hand I know, I'm one hell of a slogger!

CROSS WORDS

The words in his head are like magnets,
As they stick to his emotions like glue
He lacks the cold courage to tell her,
But knows it's the right thing to do.

He knows it will hurt her so deeply
Once again, it will break her heart
He knew it was his final warning,
Knew right from the very, very start

And now he hears her feet on the gravel
His heart is pounding as she opens the door
He buries his head in the newspaper,
She'll show him no mercy that's for sure!

So what has he done that's so very awful,
Why does he feel such terrible shame?
Because he's cracked her precious anagram
And gone and finished her crossword again!

DEAR DARLING EDDY

Before I write this letter and post it off to you
I need to pour a glass of wine, or maybe I'll have two.
Yours forever...

Dear darling Eddy
I don't know where to start; you've always been so wonderful
I love you with all my heart... (Small sip)
But lately things have seemed to change, I hope you will agree
We haven't seen eye to eye, you're right, it's must be me.
(Big sip)

I know my friend can elaborate, when she said you'd made a pass
You're right she must be lying; I need to fill my glass!
(Glug glug glug)
Would you really cheat on me, are my friend's allegations true?
Or was my internal instinct, right all along about you?
(Bigger swig)

Thinking back, there was that time, when I caught you
chatting up May
You told me I was paranoid, told me to... *"watch what I say!"*
(Empty glass)
I apologised profusely, shame on me, it wasn't your fault
I really should have known better, a liar you are not!
(New bottle)

But then, if I remember rightly,
there have been a few porky pies
Again you said I was delusional, that you'd never tell me lies
(small swig from the bottle)
You said you found her crying, she asked for your support
You said *"that she had asked for it"* pity you got caught!
(Massive swig from the bottle)

You said I was a silly cow, too emotional to see, that you would
never take advantage, particularly of me!
Like an idiot I believed you, turned my back on all my friends
They said you were a controller and would hurt me in the end!

Like a fool I didn't believe them kept on going back for more
(massive massive swig from the bottle)
My makeup covered the bruises; you knocked me to the floor!
(Crying into the bottle)
Oh Eddy you're right as always, what an idiot I have been
Not to see right through you, an evil monster machine!

And now as I drink the last dregs I have total transparency
(dries her eyes)
You're one abusive lying cheater, it's over, stay away from me
'Cos if you don't take me seriously I'm going to kill you
deader than dead
By using my empty wine bottle and smashing it over your head!
(Hic hic hic ha ha ha)
Yours no longer ...

DECONSTRUCTED NURSERY RHYMES

Hey there fiddle do you know...
The dish brought back the spoon
The little dog no longer laughs
At the unmasked cow on the moon...

The cat no longer sits on the mat
And Bo beep has found her sheep
The old woman has left the shoe
And has no more children to keep

Jack sprat now eats his fat
And the pussy is out of the well
Mary, Mary is still contrary
And refuses to use her Gel

IT COULD BE YOU!

Go on, don't worry, it won't happen to you...
Pour another drink; eat a cake or two...
Lie back on the sofa; turn up the heat...
Take care of yourself, you deserve a treat!
Get comfy, relax, and kick off your shoes...
A heart attack you say, no not you!
Recycle the diet; don't skimp on the fat...
Enjoy yourself Matey, what's wrong with that?
No need for exercise, you've years left yet...
Throw away the trainers, come on, no threat!
Zumba's for dancers, Yoga's a bore
Pilates over rated, does nothing for your core...
Anyway, stop worrying; you've nothing to fear...
You're young and healthy, open another beer.
Light up that cigarette, swill down the wine...
Top up the salt, you're looking real fine...
What's that you say I can't really hear...?
You've a pain in your chest, becoming severe...
No, not you, it's indigestion for sure
Sit down, deep breathe, you're hitting the floor!
What's that you're saying you're starting to whine...?
You're looking real sweaty, you're on the decline
You've a pain in your arm, you're feeling real sick
The pressure on your chest feels like a brick!
I really can't believe it, it's undeniably true
Oh no! A heart attack...it could be you!

LADIES LAUGHING OVER LUNCH

Here we are, together again, ladies laughing over lunch
Friends for over sixty years, still the same crazy bunch
We decided to meet at Gibson's, waited for the other three
Dee was in the car park her bare backside for all to see
She'd been to her weekly exercise and needed to get dressed
Chris used her longline cardigan to hide her knickers and vest
Mary was there before us had arrived a little too soon
So she bought herself a cuppa and sat in the other room
Eventually we united, our stomachs were rumbling free
Dee ate enough for all of us even shared Ches's cream Tea!
Chomping like we'd never eaten, swapping crisps and jams alike
Oblivious to the other customers,
we must have looked a funny sight
The poor waitress dropped some crockery,
her face paled with fear
Dee, as though still in school, clapped loudly,
gave a hearty cheer
I think Dee realised all too soon it was behaviour from the past
She said it was just spontaneous, oh, how we all laughed!
If only I could bottle the chemistry that makes us feel so young
Each time we meet, it's just as though our friendship's
just begun
There's never enough time for conversation,
always so much to say
We could continue speaking forever, and still need another day
Reminicse about our history, our worries then
few and far between
The main concerns were our eruptions,
the biggest spots ever seen

Or was it the nits found by the nurse,
the sucking crawlies of the night
Clinging on to us like leaches, our hair, not a pretty sight
The use of the spiteful metal comb, and the smell of the TCP
Both of them were so torturous, there was simply no amnesty
But we were all brought up together; we learnt how to be tough,
No room for feeling sorry for ourselves, at times we had it rough
Like working hard at fifteen and tipping up all of our wages,
Not much chance to save any, and if we did it took us ages
So we'd sit in the legion, and drink a pint through the use
of straws,
Always shared half of nothing, this was Aylesham laws
Never bearing any Malice; we learnt to manage our money well
On Friday night down the Ratling, now there's a story to tell
One of us would buy a ticket and then go straight to the loo
Then open up the window for the rest of us to climb through
We looked like something from the great escape,
tumbling to the floor
Our thighs were always black and blue,
and scarred for ever more
Yes The Ratling club was where we danced, and played the
teenage game
Not knowing then the time we shared would never come again
Just young girls, no cares in the world, we were riding our
ponies high
Margate Ballroom, the Sound House, Toffs
not forgetting the Bally Hai
We'd never pay our train fares, just repeated the same old game
One of us bought a ticket, the rest would jump on to the train.
Then when Chris passed her test we would play
the same old stunt
In her attempt not to pay at the Toll Gate,
she hit the car in front

Oh those days come flooding back as we order another cup of tea
Still laughing our silly old heads off, at how things used to be!
We all felt so wonderfully safe, the Aylesham lads kept us near
Always kept an eye on us, we never had anything to fear!
So comparing our lives to what was then; spotty years now gone
We know we will stay together always singing the same old song
For our lives, like our memories, are linked,
no matter how hard we try
Not forgetting Bena, Chippy and Sue,
in our hearts, until we die.
And now we are back to present day, respectful
and not at all deranged
Grown up, matured mothers and grandmothers
yes, we have really changed
So as we swallow our last piece of roll, the time has finally come
For one of us to pay the bill and the rest of us to run!

LAST WISHES

When I am dead and gone
Keep my love in your pocket
Please don't smother me
By placing my ashes in a locket.

LIFE OF A SHOE

Consider this, the life of a shoe
What it feels like to be under you
Visiting places, it may not like
Exhausted and battered a terrible life.

Sticking to chewing gum, wading through poo
There is no amnesty, it's all about you!
Bombarded with stones, tickled by feathers
Abused all their life, synthetics or leathers

They remain invisible, carrying your weight
Not knowing their future, dreading their fate
They exist to keep you happy, Mr Winter boot
Mrs Summer sandal, bright colours to suit

Never complaining when you buy the wrong size
Your overlarge feet squeezed tightly inside
Then when they're old and the soles worn thin
You simply take them off, and stuff them in the BIN!

LONG LOST FAMILY!

We're off to Ireland our family has been found
Thanks to Brother John, for breaking new ground!
Spent years checking records, to ensure he's right
Sourced the Morriss's on the famous Ancestry site

After so long of wondering where we belonged
My clever, generous brother had tethered a bond
So we booked our flights and off we all went
John stayed behind, he was too overspent.

For Dublin is expensive, like London Town
Particularly the Guinness, we all guzzled down
However, it didn't matter, we seized the day
Connecting to our roots, yes it was a long way!

Worth it for our family, doing the right thing
Traipsing off to Tipperary to meet our cousin Win
We walked up to her window, she was snoring fast asleep
We tried to gain her attention, she slumbered far too deep.

So we banged upon her window, KNOCK KNOCK KNOCK!
She nearly died before our eyes; we gave her such a shock!
"Who are you?" she gasped, as we shook her reluctant hand
We are your long lost family, she could barely understand

I don't think I know you; please tell me your name...
The same as yours we echoed, we were back in the game
We shared a nice hot cuppa; we had found our long lost Kin!
We posed for the album, our Iris me and our Win...

She asked if we'd send photos, if only we had known
The news we would be faced with when we arrived back home
No extended family welcomes and no history in the making
John had researched the wrong family, been annoyingly
mistaken

So we had almost killed a stranger, an eighty year-old at that
By knocking on her windows, waking her from her nap
Why did we do it... of course we did it for him
Traipsed off to Tipperary...on our John's stupid whim!

But this is not the end of Win she plans to visit us soon
She's asked to stay with John, stay in his spare room
She has her flights booked ready; she knows that we all care.
Especially our John who has paid for a complete strangers fare!

THE MONSTER

There's been a Monster seen in Eastry,
around the crack of dawn
It's supposed to have two heads, and sneaks across the lawn
They can't tell if it's human, for there's hair all over its face
They say it's been down Lower Street, but no one gives it chase
So I thought I'd trap the Monster, I thought I'd lie in wait
I got up extra early; I never sleep in late…
Then just as I was leaving, I was filled with an awful dread
Had the phantom caught me out I slowly turned my head
And then I finally realised as I stood without a sound
The phantom was my eldest son doing his paper round.

MRS HOUSE PROUD

When did my hands become dusters?
When did my legs become remote?
When did I start wearing a necklace?
Of bleach bottles around my throat!

When did the vacuum start asking?
Demanding to share my duvet
When did the mop start moaning?
Of not being washed every day!

When did the windows start screaming?
They needed their nets to be cleaned
Motivating the parched wooden table
To ask for polish to keep it creamed

When did I become Mrs House Proud?
When did I marry myself into hell?
I guess it was during the lock down
I said "I do" to Mr. Antibacterial Gel!

MY FAIRY

When she arrives I feel the need to curtesy
I take my seat; I am at my fairy's mercy
I tell her how I like it, she listens with intent
Ok a bit off here, a bit there, we start to vent
We talk about everything from holidays, to grief
I don't know how she does it, beyond belief,
I hope she works her magic, she has creative flair
Use topiary on my Barnet, a duck, I am a daft mare!
I think she's ignored me; the magic wand is in use
She has her own agenda, she's been let loose!
Cut here, smoothing down, little bit more off there
It's cracking ok for her; it's not her precious hair!
Oh! my word what will I look like, heaven forbid
If she's cut it to her liking, I might have to get rid.
Now the final viewing, oh! It's nothing like I asked
She's done her own thing again, but wait, quite surpassed
It looks a bit shorter than normal; my face don't look so fat
I'm glad my Fairy ignored me, love it, thank goodness for that!

MY FRIEND

My friend, it's true, life is changing fast,
So look to the present, and let go of the past.
It's time for new beginnings, you're ready and free,
People will gasp! It's not her, it can't be!

Strip off the pyjamas, dressing gown and rug,
Tart up your image, ditch the shrug.
Wear high heeled shoes instead of the flats,
Paint the town red, wear those purple hats.

Sport bright coloured eye-shadow, powder and paint,
Your shocking behaviour will make people faint,
Let go of your inhibitions, the big drawers have gone,
Dig out your old suspenders, stockings, and a thong.

A right foxy lady with a brand new image,
Independent and confident, to shock the village!
But wait; what's wrong, you can't go you say?
Of course I forgot, it's our Botox day!

MY RIVAL

You'd know him if you saw him, he's harmless to be fair
Smiling and smirking, he sits on the bedroom chair
He has my latest book in hand, he can't read a line
He really looks so nonchalant; he's one of a kind
He wears his own colours, red, black, yellow, and white
I suppose he's quite beguiling, a comforting sight
You tell him all your secrets, kiss him more than me
Sometimes he's on your pillow, strange sight to see
I swear I'll get my own back, unravel him for sure
Then throw him in the wardrobe behind the bedroom door
So who is my rival that lives without a care?
Of course it's dear old Rupert, your tatty old knitted bear.

NEST EGGS

No wind to blow my cobwebs away
No new broom to sweep them clean
Like a fool, I counted my chickens
I thought I was living the dream!

I suffered those con men so gladly
I paid costly and joined their ride
I was wrong to use just one basket
Not all of my nest eggs survived!

I turned to my trusted adviser
She said, it was time that I learnt
If I continued to play with the fire
Then I would most probably get burnt!

So "goodbye" to those risky, investments
And "hello" to safe banking once more
My nest eggs are tucked in my mattress
And will hatch into chick chicks for sure!

NURSERY RHYME NONSENSE

Humpty Dumpty had reconstructive surgery
All the kings' horses and king's men gave a cheer
Little Miss Muffet had counselling on her tuffett
Now she and the spider have nothing to fear

Sing a song of sixpence has gone up with inflation
So has the cost of the cereal, oats and rye
Blackbirds need to preserved for prosperity
So Quorn meat is substituted in the king's pie

Little Bo Peep has found her naughty sheep
On a packed ferry going over to France
The animal protesters were still on board
And thankfully rescued them just by chance

Jack and Jill managed to get up the hill
As fast as their bodies could caper
The rock a bye baby had a bump on its head
So Jill bathed it with Jacks vinegar and brown paper

Little Jack Horner was not in his corner
And he hadn't eaten all of his pie
He was helping Polly put the kettle on
And saying what a good boy am I

Polly told Sukey to put her thumb in the pie
Sukey was afraid she'd pull out jack's Plum
Jack hid his head in Miss Muffet's Tuffet
What was happening what had things become?

Then just in time the old woman appeared
She had with her Sam's old frying pan
She quickly rescued Jack from Polly
And his plum from greedy supping old Nan

The three men in the boat got wind of this
And rowed as fast as they could
Sadly they didn't get very far
They were eaten by the wolf in the Hood

NO RHYME OR REASON

There is no rhyme or reason, excuse the pun
In the order my poems decide to come
They can be therapeutic, sad, funny or direct
Spoken to me whenever, in any given dialect
I view them as a medicine, I need a daily dose
They increase my serotonin, stop me being so morose
Like them or hate them, I really don't care
To deny them a voice, would be so unfair
So I will keep on writing and sharing them too
Whether you delete or save is entirely up to you!

OMICRON VARIANT

So here it is again wearing a different disguise
Surely it can't fool us, as we must now realise
If we are to keep each other safe and avoid lock down
We need to have the booster to stop it spreading around
We all have a moral duty, to protect our N.H.S.
Already under pressure, and oh so much duress
So come on all you people, take heed to what I say
Keep yourself protected, and live another day!

PLASMA V PLASTIC

Are we so different to the computer that sits on the study desk?
Is this thought questionable, even fanciful, no less?
I suppose we could consider, before we throw the idea out
That we both process data, sifting it in, sifting in out!

We both have a hard drive, although, ours is called a heart,
We couldn't live without it, wouldn't even start
Of course we speak and sing, but we can't cut and paste
We can't deliver emails but we can use track and trace...

We can't scroll back, and we can't delete out
There's no automatic recovery, agreed beyond a doubt
So what do we have in common, apart from use of a pen?
When we're dead we are dead and will never work again.

PUZZLED

Try as I may or try as I might
I can't seem to get this poem quite right
It needs to be smart it needs to be neat
It needs to have content, it needs to speak
So it hurry up, or I'll delete it for sure
And leave myself wondering, was there more.

SHOES ON STRIKE

Oh no! What's happening, my shoes have gone on strike,
They've tied their laces together and dug their heels in tight.
They said they want more polish, not forgetting new soles
and heels,
No time for negotiations, no wriggle room, no last ditch appeals!

They are tired of being neglected, in the box, without a fix
Stretched to their limits, size seven squashed into a size six!
Proclaimed they are no longer needed,
hardly see the light of day
No exercise, no nourishment, why do I treat them in this way!

The trouble is they are out of date, just simply not in fashion
They didn't take this in their stride, said I have no compassion
Tired of me taking liberties and have now walked out the door
To wait inside the recycle bin to be loved again once more!

SHOES

I squeezed my foot into your shoe
To see what I could do for you
I wriggled my toes and empathised
Couldn't make sense of all those lies...
Where did they come from?
Where did they go...?
I don't suppose I'll ever know
So I'll leave your shoe and its lingering pong
And return to mine, where I belong

TEXT SPEAK

OMG txtspk is evrywhr
Teachrs are concerned
4 y dey don't do it
But the've all learnt
It's NBDEAL TBHonest
And FWIW, TMRW is another day
So rlax evry1, 4 AFAIK, txtspk is here 2 stay

Oh my gosh! Text speak is everywhere
Teachers are concerned
For they don't do it
But they have learnt
It's no big deal, to be honest
And for what it is worth
Tomorrow is another day
So relax everyone for as far I know
Txtspk is here to stay, hey ho!

THE BATH TUB

It's got to go it's had its day, surely you must see
She hears them scoff, go away, leave me be!
I'm not giving it up, because I love it so
It's expensive and frivolous, surely you know

It's took me years to have one all on my own
She had to share with her sisters, when at home
Get a shower, it's , so much cheaper to run
Not nearly so comfortable, and far less fun!

You're a grown woman now; fun's a thing of the past
You need to preserve your water and make it last
Well if that's your attitude I think it sucks
And what on earth will I do with all my ducks!

THE BATTLE OF THE NUMBER PLATES

HRT 6 and ALPHA 8,
Dashing by, there's no time to wait.
Zipping to the left, dodging to the right
Like rabid dogs, they're ready to fight.
Look out! Wait; get out of my lane!
Fist are raised, so much to gain,
Teeth are bared, the gloves are off
"I was here first," you can hear them scoff!
I'm not having this, you, overtake me!
We'll see about that, just wait and see.
Get out of my way, I've had enough,
This metal jungle is far too rough!
The foot's gone down, they're on their way
They've left the car park for another day!

THE BIRTH OF LINDA MORRISS

When I was born I disappointed my brother
He didn't want me he cried to my Mother
He needed a boy for moral support
A girl was inconceivable perish the thought!

Alas he realised for or worse
He couldn't send me back there was no reverse
I was here for good I was his fourth sister
Our John had his heart set more on a Mister

My outnumbered brother smothered by girls
Perfume and makeup jewellery and curls
He had no escape what could he do
Thought of a way, yes he knew...

Oh this was bliss not a sister in sight
To chat to a man was sheer delight
So what did he do that now seems so barmy
Yes, you guessed it, our John joined the army!

THE DUKE'S WELLIES

We stare at his boots, they know his story
Protected his toes, when he blazed in the glory
They now stand alone, legless, at his bed
More famous than the Duke, he's long dead!

THE HOARDER!

I really need to do this, I've been threatening for a while
I've turned into a hoarder and they've turned into a pile
I know it might seem simple, to throw them all away
Had some of them since schooldays, what more can I say

There are many different occasions, and I can list them all
Birthday, Anniversary, Christmas, too many to recall
They all seem far too beautiful to be tossed in the recycling bin
Not forgetting their enormous cost, it seems such a sin!

So please tell me what to do, as I deliberate the fate of my cards
Throwing away, a lifetime of love, is proving far too hard
So I'll put them back in their boxes, keep them safe until I die
Then watch my family light the biggest bonfire from my place
within the sky!

THREE SCORE YEARS AND TEN

I don't know too much about being seventy
Because I am still a very "fittish" sixty nine
I have no intentions of going out to grass
Perish the thought; I'm just in my prime!
There will be no "shopper on wheels" for me
Or people taking my arm to cross the road
No riding on stair lifts and mobility aids
I would sooner crawl upstairs with my load!
I won't be wearing that obtrusive hearing aid
It feels like a brown boil stuck behind my ear
Or glasses that make me look like a "piggy"
I am not going to suffer them, far too severe!
I will be out on the town, enjoying myself
Sampling a few cocktails and fruity gins
Be the first in the pub and the last to leave
Self-preservation, I'm not giving in!
Maybe this is about being stubborn
And not wanting to put pride into my pocket
However, if I fail not to act my age
My ashes will be off to space, with Elton
In his rocket!

THE POST MORTEM

So here we are, it's almost over, the parting of the ways
There is no need for pen and paper, as in the olden days
The need to lick a stamp has gone, posting a thing of the past
Poor Queen Atossa of Persia thought letter writing would last!

At fifty she wrote the first letter, in the year five hundred BC
It's unknown what was in it, but it was important, obviously
So now, as I use my email, I am condoning the death
of the letter
I'm not as educated as Queen Atossa, but
I really should know better!

THE SCRAP BOOK

A snap shot in time in a book full of love,
Can change the mood on a day that feels black.
Just open the pages and let yourself read
The memories will come flooding back!

Photos and tickets of holidays long gone
Suitcase labels, old passports and Fetes.
Weddings and serviettes, autographs, and cards
Not forgetting the excitement of blind dates.

So many treasures of special times gone by
Just looking at them will make your heart sing!
A keepsake of life that will never come again
Shame you can't remember one blooming thing!

THE SHINY RED STAR

It didn't happen very often, in fact, hardly ever, at all
But when it did the joy it brought was a pleasure to recall
To turn the page in my maths book and see the shiny red star
Is as ecstatic as the memory of buying my very first car!

THE TALE OF TWO TEETH

We were sat in "Chippers" Cinema
Mary called "I've lost my teeth"
I quickly plonked my "tub" down
And rummaged beneath my seat!
Mary was beside herself,
She was, lisping all the while
Meeting her new date "toothless"
Was clearly not her style!
Meticulously I dredged the floor,
But nothing could be found
I had paid to watch the film,
Left her to it, sat back down!
Oh, please don't stop looking,
She exposed a gritted gum
The boys will be here soon
What happens when they come?
I selfishly ignored her pleas
Which echoed round the room?
I tucked into my ice-cream" tub"
Went to lick the end of the spoon
And that is when I found them
Covered in my chocolate sauce
They must have fallen in my tub
I laughed till I was hoarse
Mary gave a sigh of relief
"You found them just in time"
Only then to realise...The teeth I found were mine!

THREE LITTLE WORDS

He's the king of his castle and he lends himself well
To maidens and fables and tales that tell…
Of happiness and sadness and cold coffee cups
And smoking and drinking he's down on his luck!

Three little words, do not disturb,
Hang round his neck, like the label
He's plenty of ink but he can't seem to think
Of how the knight will rescue his Mable

Three little words, do not disturb
That hides the cracks in his armour
Mabel's long gone, like the words of his song
And he needs a knight to come, find her…

Three little words, do not disturb
His "baccy" tin shows him no favours
He longs for a smoke and maybe a joke
As his mind gives him no words to save her

Three little words he's losing the plot
Will he have no end to his fable?
He picks up his pen, he can do it again
And searches for the end, he is able

He charges his phone, he feels so alone
As he watches his text slowly sending
Come back to my life, my beautiful wife
He wins the hand of his maiden!

She's proud of her knight; he put up a fight,
And he freed himself from the label
Three little words…Do not disturb
He's off to make love to his Mabel…

TOM CAT

I think Tom's at it again; he's just sneaked out the door
He's tightened up his collar and preened his coat for sure
His punchy paws are pristine clean; his head is held up high
He knows just where he's going; I can't stop him if I try
Because he's off to eat his supper, it really breaks my heart
She says she is my friend, been after him from the start
Calling him down the alley, her fluffy tail swinging high
Those flashy green eyes, lighting up the evening sky
Charmed him with her beef, wooed him with her chicken
I am left to eat the lettuce, limp, definitely not paw licking
Oh Tom, you need to remember or you'll be out on your ear
for sure
That we are vegetarians, the carnivores live next door!

WHO DIED?

It is not like me to be so judgemental
But surely, you're not wearing that dress?
Looks like it needs a dam good ironing
Oh dear, look at you, what an awful mess!

It seems I arrived not a minute too soon
For I am known for my very good taste
Do you think you might need to wear a belt?
To support your thickening waist

And have you forgot the well-known rhyme
About black and blue will never, ever do
Even if it is just for someone's funeral
What are you thinking, shame on you!

And honestly, what's up with your hair,
It looks so untidy and far too bright
I guess it was an overdose of the peroxide
Oh dear, it really is far too light

And surely not those inappropriate shoes
If you slip you'll be sure to lose an eye
Why not borrow my sensible brogues
Come on, try them on now, and don't be shy!

I dread to think what's coming next
Oh, surely not that dated open collar coat
Here take my real woollen scarf;
It'll hide your scraggy old throat

So tell me "hotch pot" who did you say died?
Come on now big girl voice, no need to cry
Is it someone I know? Or is it that awful man
Give you three guesses BANG! BANG! BANG!

WHO IS THIS WOMAN?

She's held together with some rusty old screws
Helping her make those dodgy old moves
An old replacement knee, a bandaged wrist
Repetitive strain from the jive and the twist
There's grey in her hair, it clogs up the sink
The perm has long gone, no need for the "TWINK"
Her eyesight has dimmed, or the needle's too small
Her hearing is failing, she misses her calls
She's patient and kind, conscientious and free
An amazing woman, anyone can see...
She's caring and empathic, some may say quaint
But let me tell you... the ladies no saint
She may have fooled many, but she don't fool me
I can see right through her, there are lots to see
From dusk to dawn she's out on the town
Drinking and dancing, hanging around...
The police know her personally she's a pest
Looks an unbecoming sight in her psychedelic vest
Her brightly coloured hair can be seen from space
Purple ears, purple neck, it's even on her face!
Her bright red lips are smudged from the gin
She has her own cocktail called "madam sin"
Oh yes she is a handful, I know you'll agree
So who is this woman, well now, you tell me!

WOULD YOU?

If you were offered the opportunity, to go back
and erase the time
Change the parts of your life that didn't always rhyme
Would you?
If you could conquer all the fears that brought so many tears
Preventing you from enjoying happy times throughout the years
Would you?
If you could live with total sobriety
without the pressures of society
Allowing you the freedom to be congruent,
yourself entirely
Would you?
If you could scale and conquer the highest mountain,
And drink from the sweetest, fullest fountain
Would you?
Or are you thankfully content, knowing the life you've spent
Is as near perfect for you as Lois Lane is for Clarke Kent?

THE CAT-ASTROPHE!

Bored... *"Hm, not too bad"*... he wonders what her name is.
Pretty eyes, urgent smile, beginning to eat out of his hand
Definitely more interested than an hour ago, *"Hello you"*
She responds to him, how warm she feels, snug, like a bug
He's fallen, smitten, something is stirring, and he strokes her hair
He wonders how much she is, how many weeks pocket money
*"Come on son, you can't afford her she is way too expensive,
no contest"*
He sighs and watches, as though she knows,
she is already sat on another's lap.

Seasons

THE RAZZMATAZZ OF SPRING

As winter throws of its overcoat,
and prepares to greet the sun
Daffodils blow their trumpets, as though heralding
what's to come
Proud trees dress for the occasion,
refreshed with the morning dew
A chorus of faithful violets, harmonise with the bells so blue
A colourful extravaganza, as the whole world begins to sing
Welcoming the colour burst
and the glorious razzmatazz of spring

SUMMER'S MOVING IN

It's time to do some decluttering said Mother Nature
to fading Spring,
You've had your three months of glory,
now Summer's moving in.
It's time to pull out Jack in the Pulpit
and replace him with Canna Lily
Dead head the Christmas rose, the Iris;
they are looking rather silly.

Tie up the King Alfred Daffodils; salute
the pretty Queen of the Prairie,
Push out the Pussy Willow, the Crab Apple,
and prune old Rose Mary.
Make room for Black Eyed Susan, Flowering Tobacco
and Sneezeweed,
Not forgetting the purple Petunia and the Sun Flower
grown from seed.

Say goodbye to dear old Crocus, and hello
to the proud Hydrangeas
Leave the Hosta, and the Buddleia, still snug
in their bright containers.
And when these chores are completed
and your garden's ready for fun
You'll be the first to greet the Summer
and feel the warmth of her sun!

AUTUMN

Here she is again with her enormous arms outspread
Gathering up the remains of summer and putting it to bed
Spurring on September, wake up; it's your time to shine
Parade your golden russets, amorous ambers and reds divine!

A time to harvest abundantly, a time to spread joy and love
Turning the blue skies to delicious sunsets way up above
Breezing in a magnitude of yellows, browns, an autumn feast
Teasing our eyes, like some huge banquet,
temptation unleashed!

A fanfare of optimism, dancing shadows on the window sill
A swirling of things to come, the never ending timeless chill
Mother Nature doing her job, the   seasons own care taker
Not knowing what's to come, for that's the role of The Maker.

THE WINTER QUEEN

Here she comes, wearing her magnificent white gown
Her hair spiked with icicles, "Winter Queen's" back in town
Brace yourself, for this lady plays an important part
Being the last in the Seasons, she has no warming heart!
No empathy is shown to the shrivelling Hydrangeas
As they hide their roots, deep, in their cosy containers
She waves to fragile Pansies, for their role is done
They need to sleep, recuperate, and wait for the March sun
She embraces them in her cold, captivating arms
Be careful; do not fall for her empowering deadly charms
The driven snow, the biting, morning chilly air
She's in cahoots with the wind, they cause such despair
Blowing the last of the petals and leaves from the trees
The Queen shows no mercy, ignores their shivering pleas
She has no other intention her job is to preserve, not give in
So that Spring will rejuvenate as a new year cycle begins.

Love and Emotion

ABANDONMENT

As she clutched on forlornly, a small child of two
Bereft of her mother and her father now too
No room in the home, for a child so young
The silent piano, her score unsung
At the mercy of another, wrapped within a shawl
Knew not where she was going, knew nothing at all
Abandonment, sacrifice, snatched from his arms
To be given to a stranger, a tarnished lucky charm.

AND NOW THEY ARE GONE

And now they are gone and they are missed
So many who were here, now no longer exist
Except in our memories, photos and our hearts
Kept alive so passionately, cruelly death parts

We can never fill the space; it's a cold empty hole
It freezes our mind, our body, weakens our soul
We try to fight it, convince ourselves we are ok
Lie about our feelings to fool the endless day

For there is no antidote for pining and the rawness of pain
Knowing they are all gone and will never come again
The physical ache of the yearning, the tears that don't flow
Such a sickening, sobering clarity, where did they go

They were here just now, laughing, breathing, so strong
And then with one last precious heartbeat, they were gone!

BLAMED

She's bleeding painful memories for the years long gone
Resurrected by the   malicious hounds, the hunt goes on
Stabbing knives of pain, penetrating steel, so icy cold
Sharp shocks of disappointment, piercing her frozen soul

She must deserve it, she procrastinates, disturbs the rot
Ruminates, self-depreciation, kind to herself, she is not
She knows where it has come from, this cruel hand of fate
The distorted memories, the fragile scab, a ghost to placate

CHALKY BOULDERS

When I was small he'd make me tall, by sitting me
on his shoulders
And when I cried he'd dry my eyes, play chucks
with chalky boulders.
He spoke to me about rabbits and dogs
and birds that flew in the sky
Showed me how to draw a house, was attentive,
till time crept by.
Then the day came, I knew it would, he left me to join the army
I missed him so, couldn't let go,
I didn't take the news very calmly.
Can still recall, when his leave was due, how I would try
to stay awake
There were times I managed to do this,
other times he was far too late.
And on his visits home, my heart would almost burst with joy
He'd bring me home nationality dolls, was a kind generous boy.
Yes, no other was like my brother,
he meant the whole world to me
And anyone, who knew us well, would passionately agree.
Special memories will remain in my head,
until the day I leave this earth
But wait just a moment; my sister said
something happened at my birth!
She said he wanted to send me back,
said he didn't want another sister
Slapped me on my bum and said disdainfully
he wanted me to be a mister

How hurt I felt, to hear this news
it was a crushing wounding blow
The brother I had worshipped, how awful,
he would have let me go!

But then I suppose I would have felt the same
if I had wanted a mister
I understood his frustration
the only boy in a house full of sisters
And now I have grown, and he's forgiven,
and I'm too old to sit on his shoulders
But we are still as close as when we were young,
playing chucks with chalky boulders.

BUCKET LIST

There are so many things people choose to do
Writing memoirs, painting, downsizing too
Reliving old memories, revamping photo books
Exhausting visits to the gym to tighten up one's looks!

Experience exotic holidays, visit other lands
Savour the different cuisine, sizzle on white sands.
Escape with the birds, get stung with the bees
Learn to read the Tarot cards, hug the forest trees

Learn a new skill; attend a well-being course
Take a gamble, bingo, back that winning horse
Cocktails, Spas, hot tubs and theatre thrills
Surviving in the jungle, a day out with bear grills

Yes, so many things to embrace, on a bucket list
Each of them important, nothing must get missed
But the most exciting wish, top of the page for me
A bag of chips on the pier, a pickled egg thrown in for free!

CHARLIE

Oh how I love my many beds
With my favourite cuddly toy
Snuggled within my blankets
I'm such a lucky boy
To think I was a rescue
Saved from an awful place
Now I'm safe and loved
By a couple called Tiny and Trace

CONSCIENCE

It seeks no pity, in the confinement of the cage
Held together by guilt, trapped and enraged
Entangled, knotted, through the years it seeps
Like an unhealed sore it festers and weeps.
Slowly decaying like dead meat in the sun
Finally, rotting away,   the damage is done!

EBBING OF THE TIDE

The waves massage the shore line, like the hands of a skilled
masseuse
Some pebbles become well rounded, others remain rough,
loose.
But the sea keeps on pounding until the rough become smooth
too
The ebbing of the tide, eventually, will do the same for me and
you!

ENTER AT YOUR PERIL

The house on the hill, has a nailed up door,
No one dare enter, it's barred for sure.
Demons and enemies sleeping like logs,
Try not to wake the rabid old dogs.

The story is unknown; it's been a mystery for years
Shrouded in pain, awkwardness and tears.
Enter at your peril, tread the bare mat,
Remember though, what happened to the cat.

Trees grow through windows, gnarled and brown
People say it's haunted by a lady in a gown
They were lovers I hear say, but trouble loomed
Betrayal and heartbreak, they were doomed.

Scandal and shame a life time's curse
Permanent, set in stone, like an indelible verse.
So stay well away if you treasure your life
Think wisely, is it worth it; go home to your wife.

GANGSTER GRANNY COOL

To see their smiling faces looking back at me
Captures my heart and soul with warm pride
I'm so blessed to have so many of them
So privileged to walk, and laugh at their side

They include me in all their special times
Christmas, Birthday, Easter and school
Confide in me about how they are feeling
I'm known as Gangster Granny cool

Of course, the title comes with a responsibility
Which clearly means I'm obliged to play
At dress up, draughts, dolls and make believe
In any minute of any hour of any given day

There is no room for me to say I am busy
Or we'll do it when the next time you visit
No opportunity for me to bribe or compromise
If I can't say yes, then quite candidly I miss it

So speaking from many, many years of experience
Enjoy whatever your grandchildren ask you to do
Eventually, the time you spent investing in them
Will be returned in abundance, from them to you.

HOW DARE I

How dare I criticise another,
particularly the one I know as Mother?
She had no rules to guide her as she slipped from child t'other.
Married at sixteen to my Father
she was just a young teenage bride
No Mother did she have to love her or stand by her side.

She learnt from those around her being given away
at the age of two
In a fish shop known as Ben's by her Father
who didn't know what to do!
Her Mother's death was so sudden,
left her Father with a brood of four
It gave a shock to all the family
when death knocked unannounced on the door.

The family fell into a trauma;
they were ruptured at the very seams,
No more gathering around the organ and singing
of far off dreams.
The two sisters went to service and her brother
to a manager's home
My Mother was sent to live with The Rees's
frugal love to her was shown.

Although Ben was far kinder than Mary,
as to her my Mother was a prop,
A golden haired child trophy,
to be paraded to all who entered the shop.
She treated my mother so badly,
like one of those monkeys on a stick,
Ne cuddles or offers of love, just beatings
and spiteful, nasty tricks!

She had such a sad, lonely, life, rejected again
at the age of eight
Sat there waiting for Mother Mary,
who never walked back through the gate
So should I criticise my mother
for the way she always treated me?
No, I have no right to criticise my mother,
and my children, no right to criticise me!

HAPPY AS LARRY

"How are you" I'd call as I opened the door
"I'm ok" came the cheery reply.
"I could do with a cuppa when you get time"
She croaked through lips that were dry.
"Enough about me, how are you..."
Her words travelled the length of the hall!
Bent over her walker, like a rag doll,
She would never, ever grumble at all!
The pain, was so clearly etched on her face,
Like the fine carvings on an old wooden chair.
Beads of cold sweat clung to her neck,
And the restless night had tangled her hair!
Never to complain she mastered her game,
Kept it under wraps like a bunion in a shoe
I protected her façade, the best way I should,
Played her game, was the least I could do.
For if she grumbled and moaned whilst with her friends,
She was frightened they wouldn't stay
So she sat with her suffering to protect her worth,
She said it was a small price to pay!
And now she's long gone, her soul is at peace,
But the laughter we shared I will carry
Her birth name was Hillary but to all her friends,
She was known quite simply as Larry!

HUMAN VOLCANO

I am sure when it happens, it will never stop
Some huge eruption, forcing its way to the top
Spilling out years of controlled emotions and pain
Ingrained, solidified lava that has never, ever waned

Passed back and forth like some old spinning yoyo
Life and living, stagnated on a permanent go go slow
No one is giving and certainly no one is taking
Just ongoing stubbornness, more garbage in the making!

I WILL MISS YOU

Lay a place for me at your table, the place where we would
sit and talk
Take me with you in the morning when you go
for the cold brisk walk
Talk to me when you feel lonely I will listen
and be right at your side
To comfort you and hold you until
the burning ache of grief subsides

Keep the last card I sent you, maybe put it
in that old silver frame
Pick it up and hold it close
if you want to feel me in your arms again
Share how you're feeling, when there's no one around to call
Wake me anytime from my endless slumber,
I won't mind at all

I know it won't be easy, we were together for many a long year
Embrace the mourning process, taste the unashamed soft tear
My darling I know you'll miss me
in the way you always do
But please do not stop living, as I would not wish that for you

So allow those tears for a little while
then dust yourself right down
Go face the world as you always did
the same when I was around
Take every opportunity; treat it as a gift to start living life anew
Take a chance on your new romance;
I hope you love him as I loved you

I'M NOT YOUR ENEMY

I am not your enemy, what have I done
Hateful and venomous, loathsome
Unconditional love, scraped from your shoe
No matter what you say, I still love you
There is no other who would take such abuse
Discrediting behaviour, deliberately obtuse!
You have wounded, maimed, I'm so overcome
I'm not your enemy, I think I'm done!

MAKE BELIEVE

I was most certain I saw you just the other day
You know where I mean, where we would play
Mothers and Fathers, my rag doll in the pram
Had a raw potato for dinner, and a slice of curled ham.

A mud pie for a pudding, a box for a table
You found a crate; we used it for a cradle
Oh such happy times, when I was your Queen
You were the best King, my eyes had ever seen.

And then we grew up and I became your wife
No longer satisfied, with our make believe life
Was it your job, late hours, or was it mine
The cold empty bed, no communication, down time

The need to have such expensive possessions
Redundancy, lost, the unexpected depression
Or was it the fact, you swapped your Queen for a King
Finally admitting, I'd just never been your thing!

MRS MAGARVEY

Mrs Magarvey sits alone…
She has no heating she has no phone
Her neighbours are young they don't understand
The strange ancient lady from a foreign land

She leaves her doors open just in case
It never seems to work, she dries her face
The loneliness like her life, black and white
Colourless, predictable, constant night

A creeping coldness seeps through her bones
Her kettle eases her unheard moans
She twitches her nets, sees more than she gets
The once owned houses now turned into lets

She is still there like a stoic oak,
She stares at her poker, she's nothing to poke
Her fire once fierce has now turned dim
She patiently waits to let her company in

She wraps her shawl tighter he'll soon be here
Her friend keeps her sane, he's nothing to fear
She searches for scraps, and fills his box
Whilst eagerly waiting, her lifeline, her fox.

PARIS ROCK CHOIR EXPERIENCE

17th-20th August 2018

We stood centre front our heads held high,
We raised our voice, we caressed the sky.
Hallelujah was strong, velvet and proud,
Tears fell unashamed, we seduced the crowd.
Notre Dame was amazing…glory be,
In a circle we sang so emotionally.
Rocking Rockies supreme, young and old
"Human" was fantastic, "More than a Feeling" gold
"Shut up and Dance" we opened our hearts
Two upper altos we learned our parts.
We clapped we sang we swayed so surreal,
And a unique time was had by two Rockies from Deal.

SADNESS

There's a place in her heart,
As cold as a stone,
Like the ice on a frozen fence
People try to warm it
There can be no recompense
Few men have tried to crack it,
With brute force, but never love
That's why it stays unbroken,
Like the dark clouds high above.

SAFE PLACE

She cast her net wide as she flowed with the tide
Gave herself up to the soothing calm sea
She danced with white horses and avoided the storm
Knowing for the first time in her life she'd be free...
She spread out her arms and surrendered her heart
Felt the wind blowing and the sun on her face...
She smiled at the clouds and the never ending peace
She'd arrived at her forever safe place...

SEEDS OF LIFE

God plants two seeds, one in the heart and one in the womb
They grow along together, and then so very soon
One seed becomes a baby, to cherish from the start
The other seed is love, growing in the heart

They grow along together, stronger by the day
The love surrounds the baby, to help it on life's way
Then all too soon the baby becomes an adult fully grown
The work is done, the seeds are shared, a baby of their own

THE AFTERMATH

And then there was a huge expanse of nothing
A gaping wound that swallowed their shared love
Unthinkable, unannounced, like death, shock!
Everything the same but now unrecognisable,
All gone, big holes, torture, a laboured life,
Never to take the same shape again, ever...
Like a baggy old jumper, or the pair of worn slippers
The cruelness of the act...The painful aftermath!

THE BAG LADY

She carries her life in a bag on her arm
Held tightly to her body, it's part of her charm
Like an uncut diamond, untouched and raw
Precious, unpolished, look inside, there's more

An old frayed lining, the contents well used
Squashed and battered, forever abused
Prejudice, hatred, assumptions and spite
Add to the monotony of her onerous fight

No abracadabra or open sesame
Will open the bag to set her spirit free
Heart wrenchingly she waits, end of the queue,
No warmth, no surprises, and no I love you

THE CHOKER

His love is like a string of pearls
Hung tightly around her throat
If he pulls on them too roughly
She's sure that she will choke
Then why won't she release them
Like a dog from some taut leash
The choker feels more comfortable
Then the wrath of his untamed beast

THE COST OF A PINT

Number 45

Yes. It's so much cheaper and there's nothing to compare
I can buy it from my local, anytime, anywhere!
I have no need to worry, about the birds and their beaks
Or it being taken by a reveller, when a drink they seek
Of course it makes sense; I will call and cancel tomorrow
Apart from number 39, I am sure the rest will follow!
They definitely won't miss him, and it will save them money
I'm wondering why he's lasted this long, seems rather funny!!!

Number 39

Has anyone heard him, for he is nowhere to be seen?
He usually brings the eggs; you know the one I mean
Up before the crack of dawn, puts the sun   to shame
Reliable and oh so friendly, I hope he comes again
Number 45's saying things, I really do not like
About saving money and cancelling, he has no right
This would be a travesty for he's the reason I survive
Brings me my potatoes, my dinner, keeps me alive!
He's always such a great support, and on him I can depend
For he's not just a milkman; he is my lifeline, a real god send
So go shopping in your garage 45,
go buy your milk from the shop
But hands off my milkman, he's the only friend I've got.

THE LAST ACT

When your script is failing and you struggle to hold on
What would you do, just stop reading ... all is gone
Or do you celebrate in what was once your pleasure
And prepare yourself to let go of another's treasure

It is a real dilemma, not as simple as just letting go
Of course, you know this already, its part of the show
The curtains come down, there is no clapping encore
The story has been told, the end, there is no more.

THE LAST GOODBYE

As he walks slowly down the once familiar way
The wind whips up memories of another day
Blowing in his face like the sand in a storm
Reminding him sadly he was there to mourn

He quickens his step, he sees people he once knew
Their heads in a hanky, wondering why, what, who
He touches their faces and wipes the anguish away
Then holds them tightly, there's nothing he can say.

THE LAST SUPPER

If I could share just one last supper
With my dear old Mum and Dad
I wouldn't fret about the washing up
Or what food we'd need to have
I would sit quietly in their company
And listen to all they had to say
I wouldn't look at the ticking clock
Or that it's getting late in the day
I would remember to say I loved them
And how much I thanked them for
And tell myself that all too soon
They will no longer knock on my door!

THE LASTING LEGACY

What do you see from heaven above?
The hurt, the pain, the fragile love
A spiteful act so damming and harsh
The virus killed one, you split five hearts
You dealt a cruel blow, to a family you loved?
Do you not think about this from heaven above?
Are you happy now, you've destroyed it all
Your lasting legacy, a family so forlorn!

THE PRICE OF THE POPPY

It's not so much about the Poppy, but,
more about what it represents
Resurrecting life from devastation,
where the bloodiness of war was spent
At Flanders field where muck and sludge, buried death,
the wounded, the lost
A barren wilderness of lifeless souls, the price of war,
the sacrificial cost
And yet out of this field of mourning, red flowers grew tall
and proud
A duvet of red velvet poppies, blowing so quietly,
yet spoke so loud
A testament to the fifty countries that fought
so war would cease
The poppy represents our conscience and the forever hope
of peace.
It signifies our gratitude, as we wear it, with upmost respect
For the continuing bravery of our forces, and those...
lest we forget
The money raised from the poppy helps our soldiers
when in need
Managed through The British Legion, a Charity which succeeds
In working hard to raise the funds, so that veterans might live
So whatever you pay for your poppy,
it's a small price to give!

THE SURREAL REALITY

Sometimes, things seem more normal than other's
When the postman comes, or rubbish is collected
Or I take an egg from the fridge, and crack it
To make breakfast that does not get eaten
Or when I see your hat and coat on the peg
Quickly diminishing, a harsh reminder, you are dead
Not lost, not popped out, not divorced, deceased
Gone for good, no time to change things, say sorry
Or put a multitude of things right, wearing cold ashes
Never to be the same again, slowly time passes

THE UNENDING

Sometimes, a fleeting second relieves the unending
And the feeling of hopelessness, lack of acceptance
Disciplined and orderly, the same, but different,
A pretence of everything being okay knowing its's not
Like walking with your shoes on the wrong feet
Or your coat being buttoned up the wrong way
Apprehension, anticipation, tail of two faces
Looking both ways, seeing nothing, distortion
Not being able to change or put things right
Nothing ever being as familiar as it was, waste
The unending that keeps you remembering to hurt
And wondering whether the unending will ever end!

TYPE CAST

His emotions swing back and forth like a child on a swing
Almost reaching the cross bar, thoughts consume him
What did he do wrong, was he not good enough,
Always tried his best, for him, life was pretty tough!

No one can judge him; they did not walk in his shoes
He searches his archive he's looking for clues
Did he change the script, reinvent his own lines
Educated through experiences, different times

His memories are vague, but not uncomfortable
Show me perfection, life is not always wonderful
Is there no room to stop this judgement from his past?
Or will he be like the actor in the soap, always typecast.

WHY?

Her soul is screaming, and yet, eyes refuse to cry
For fear of drowning and never knowing why,
You did such a cruel thing and then escaped through death
Leaving broken pieces and children's hearts bereft...

Such a beautiful family, crushed with a will
Vengeful and hurtful, a vendetta to fulfil...
It would have been so different, now it's too late
For the deed has been done, nothing to placate...

You made them a promise, you didn't carry it through
It was nothing to do with them, it was all about you!
A long term grievance that ate away at your soul
Punishing and revengeful, you achieved your goal!

Such beautiful children, estranged and so sad
Betrayed by you, the frozen boy they called Dad
Why did you do it... such an awful thing?
Did you not know the heartache that surely it would bring...
why?

Therapy

COMFORT CUSHION

They come in all sizes, at any given time
Comfortable and reassuring, hard to define
What it is that they do, not quite sure what
Feels almost magical, please don't stop

Where once you struggled, you now see the light
The wood from the trees, such a welcome sight
You can think for yourself, the anxiety is lifting
Your thoughts are awakening, automatically shifting

From negative to positive deliciously freeing
The invisible cushion, supportive, all seeing
Empathic, non-judging, conditions   are few
There is really just one" learn to believe in you!"

It's time to let go for you are moving along
Let go of the dependency, stop hanging on
Look to the future, it's yours for the taking
Say goodbye to your cushion, a new life is waiting!

DON'T GO WITH THE FLOW

When *"I'm ok"* and *"I'm just fine"* fall
like an avalanche from your mouth
Remind yourself it's *"not ok"*
to suppress your true emotions of drouth.
There's nothing wrong in being honest,
you don't always need to be strong
Find someone who will listen, when fate decides
to string you along!

For the feeling of an empty chalice,
compounded with the emotion of guilt
Can serve to feed the fragile ego, dangerous,
suffocating, clogging silt.
Years of self-depreciating narrative, speak volumes
of self-destruct and harm
Like the accepted judgement of others
and their warped sense of outdated charm.

So stop denying yourself time to recognise
when you are not feeling your best
Be succinct... *"no, I am not okay today,"*
allow yourself the time to protest.
Practice being assertive, give yourself permission
to experience, live and grow,
Stop beating yourself up with unproven facts
and maybe learn... *not* to go with the flow.

FOR A FEW HOURS MORE

For a few hours more, or maybe a day
It would mean you could tuck a bit more away
It would pay for a new bed, or even a car
Then again you've managed ok this far!

What about new jewellery, regular hairdos
A new bag, a new facelift, perhaps a new you
Are you so hard up, or is it just an excuse
Afraid to let go, cutting the tight noose!

Spent years working, it's all you know
Like the Queen, laundry, dashing to and fro
It would be a new existence, with choices and rights
Giving yourself permission, scaling new heights!

So throw caution to the wind, take a deep breath in
Leave the job, give notice, go on, and pack it all in
You'll be glad you have, you won't even mourn
You can turn off the alarm and sleep until dawn.

Because life's not all about money, or an extra few hours
It's about quality and opportunity and smelling the flowers
So enjoy your time, lead the life that you choose
Because as we all know... if you snooze you lose!

THE LAST CAKE

Dear Friend
There's no need to be at the bottom of the pile
It can be a, dreary, thankless, cold place
Like being squashed in the smallest cupboard
Unable to breathe, to think, a blank face

What would it take for you to change?
Experience pleasing yourself once in a while
Behave in a way you consider as being selfish,
Be first in the pecking order, important, reconcile

Learn to be comfortable, being uncomfortable
Seize the opportunity, you know what to do
Be brave enough to take the last cake
It's there for the taking, so why not you!

GOOD ENOUGH MOTHER!

What would they see if I were transparent?
Scars and wounds galore,
Holes in my body like a dartboard
attached to the back of the door.
Hopefulness holds my heart in place like a cradle
supporting a child,
My composed outside exterior, bares no comparison
to the anxious inside!
A struggling lump of nothingness, deflated
like a ruptured inner tube,
I could do with a little pumping up,
and then I might magnificently elude.
The feeling of being a victim whilst sitting reluctantly
on the stale pity pot,
Spewing out a magnitude of self-blaming,
but a quitter I am definitely not!
So I'll draw my thick curtains wide open
and shake off this woeful old me,
For I am not a helpless, unworthy poor mother,
I'm as good as any mother can be!

HAND CUFFS

Don't wear your bracelet for others with charms of *"should"*
or *"must"*
For a bracelet worn for others will soon corrode, wear
and rust
Keep your links well-spaced, celebrate the ones you lose
Keep a padlock on for emergencies,
to protect the charms you choose!

HANDS OF FATE

And so you made the bold decision, did what you thought
was right at the time
So why, so many years later, are you ruminating the same
self-blaming rhyme?
You can't turn the clock back; you are not in control
of your own untold fate
So stop this procrastination, or too soon, like global warming,
it will be far too late!

The hands of the clock turn quickly; they rob you
of precious living time
Worrying about things you cannot change, so stop it,
and let yourself shine.
Let go of *"what ifs"* and *"why did I do it?"*
replace them with *"didn't I do well!"*
Give yourself a well-earned break;
get out of the continuous cycle of hell!

Ask yourself this question...
why do I keep choosing to act this way?
Thinking I am totally responsible for everything
that happens each day
There are other factors in your life that affect
the decisions you make
So take off the coat of perfection and trust
in the capable hands of fate.

MRS ANXIETY

She seeps through my bones like an infusion of dread
She can make me feel unsteady on my feet, muddle my head
My heart will pound as though an intruder is near
The adrenal keeps on pumping, when there is nothing to fear!

My palms are sweaty, my face, the colour of wet cement
I am totally inaudible, can't seem to run, can't seem to vent!
Its fight or flight time, but I am totally frozen to the spot,
Over ventilating, over exaggerating, well over the top!

Keep calm, I tell myself, there is no need to feel manic
I can do it, I can manage, there's no need for this panic
Mrs Anxiety won't last long if I just tell her I am fine
And send her back to where she came from,
until the right time!

SPLINTERS

I wonder, at times, about big splinters sitting on small shoulders
Because if not removed quickly they will soon become boulders
Unmovable, toxic, like black soot on white driven snow
A heavy, wooden overcoat, they might never, ever outgrow!

THE DIFFERENCE A DAY MAKES

What would you do if you had a day to live?
Would you spend it worrying about your will?
And what possessions you had left to give...
Or would you call in your precious loved ones
Attempt to put all lifelong grievances to rest
To pass away quite peacefully, integrity at its best
Or would you use your last window of opportunity
To deliver one final crushing cruel blow
Strike back; take revenge, there, I told you so
A fruitless churlish act, as mean as can be
Final and forever, the aftermath you won't see
So think wisely powerful will maker,
About the legacy you choose to leave behind
Will it show how much you love them,
Or leave them rejected, abandoned, resigned?

A FREE WOMAN

A sliver of hate entered her heart like an icicle cooling hot tea
She knew just where it came from, it was sent so wickedly.
He told her that he loved her, made a mockery of their vows
Could never keep the promises, pointless endless rows!

But all good idiots come to an end, and finally see the light
No more whistling, like some faithful dog, divorce is in sight!
Oh my word he couldn't believe it, the worm had finally turned
Filed for the divorce, she means it, she has finally learned.

No longer taken for granted, she now knows her place
No longer carries the chains, feels the sun on her face.
Holds her head up high, no longer bottom of the pile
Being that down trodden woman, is no longer her style.

So take back your icicle and take back your slither of hate
Take back your endless bullying, for she will no longer placate
The constant negativity, the pitying words of woe is me
Empowered, enlightened, happy, and oh so very... free!

THE NARCISSIST

We all know one, you know the kind
All sweetness and light, playing with your mind
Accusing and controlling, your strength is zapped
Yet they maintain, your paranoid, set their traps

And once you're caught there seems like no way out
In for the long haul, filling your mind with doubt
Once they have you snared, you're putty in their hands
Manipulated and moulded, worms opened, empty cans

Battered and bruised demolished and defeated
To a life of ridicule, mental and physical beatings
There can be no end to this coercive control
Wait, you have a choice, to save your own soul

They don't own you, take back your power
Become powerful, assertive, it's you finest hour
Walk away, leave, you are not glued to their hip
Maintain your course of action, captain your ship

For if you choose otherwise, you will be forever lost
In mind games and cruelty, a never ending cost
They'll never change; it's far too much fun
The Narcissist loads the bullets, you fire the gun!

THE PARK BENCH

Hello there, Hi, Bonjour, How do you do
Take a seat; tell me, how life is treating you
Not bad you say, but could be much better
Thinking of writing that closure letter
What would you do if you receive a reply?
Take it further, forget, the well's run dry
Offer to meet up, put your differences aside
Start over again, forget that they lied
Or would you take a date with me, give me a go
Great, Au revoir, Bye, see you later, Cheerio.

THE RAINBOW

There's something about a rainbow, arched within the sky,
Like a huge prop of hopefulness, so pleasing to the eye
It brightens up the darkest day, and radiates a sense of light,
An opportunity to make a wish, a chance to put things right!

THE RESCUER

And then, when he knew it was enough
He stretched out and tenderly lifted him up
Into arms that held a multitude of broken dreams
And failed expectations, and what might have been
And all because he would not slacken his grip
Allow people to captain and steer their own ship
And what if he had thought in a different way
Dismissed the night and welcomed the new day
Let the light in to shine on his starving seeds
Restore and rescue his unattended diminshed needs

THE RIGHT TO REMAIN

When people leave, or eventually die,
Life's never the same, you wonder why.
For, although they have gone, you remain
Doing what you do time and time again.

You cry, and mourn, adapt and move on.
Find another self- soother, a place to belong.
Untangle yourself from the grief and deceit
For you know, wholeheartedly, there's no gift receipt!

We are all on loan; of this we can be certain,
Eventually, like frank, we face the final curtain.
So embrace your grief, resurface, and dry your eyes,
Praise yourself immensely, you have survived

You have the right to remain, keep your place
Serve your life purpose, and do not hesitate
For life's too precious to do anything else but live
And goes too quickly like the water through a sieve.

THE VOLUNTEER

Thank you for calling today
It really warmed my heart
I don't know how to thank you
I wouldn't know where to start!

It's been such a long time
Since I've seen a friendly face
I hope you come back next week
You make my home a cosier place!.

TRUST YOUR OWN INSTINCTS

When the sun feels a little less warm
and the sky a little less bright
When your smile hides behind your fears
and hope seems out of sight
What can you do to change things,
what can you use to escape the dread?
Turn your negative thoughts to positive; dispel that monster
in your head
Because help can be just around the corner,
support for anxiety is all around
Just open your heart to healthier behaviour,
keep your feet on solid ground!
Learn to breathe more deeply, breathe in the blue
and breathe out the red
Tap the stop button on your shoulder, take a minute,
and listen to what's said
Reclaim your precious power, trust your own instinct,
and cut yourself some slack
For we pass this way once only, make it count,
you're not coming back!

Christmas

BENA'S CHRISTMAS DITTY

When you take your last breath, and sing your last song
Christmas will continue and the life of others will go on
So don't become too stressed, breathe slow and be merry
Then turn on Hugh Grant and open up the Sherry

.

CHRISTMAS 2021

Shadows swallow the last of the light
Covering the sky so cosy and tight
Draw the curtains, put on the kettle
Let us snuggle together, come hither settle
Warm up our toes on the hearth of the fire
Toss over the chestnuts, feel the desire
Walnuts, tangerines, mistletoe divine
Crackers, board games, warming mulled wine
Tantalising our senses, reviving our lost soul
Having Christmas together is the common goal
So keep using the gel to stop anything sinister
And we can all enjoy Christmas, not just the prime minister.

CHRISTMAS MEMORIES

Memories resurface, the warmth embraces me
As I admire the old relics on the new-fangled tree
Mr Acorn man with a pipe cleaner for a leg
Dangles precariously from a loop in his head

The fragile sparkly bauble, that shatters to the touch
Kid gloves needed now, cosseted so very much
Mum's pink Chinese lantern, the blue Virgin Mary
The painted wooden soldier, the glass snow fairy

A well pulled cracker, the tissue faded and flat
The joke long forgotten, all that remains is the hat
Ripped and tattered, to be treasured forever
A reminder of Mum's last Christmas, discard, never!

The sixties musical church, is still a proud sight
A red roof, sweet paper windows, all is calm all is bright
Standing on Iris's mantel, another family antique
Melodic, poignant, still winding, sounds so sweet

So many nostalgic memories, of the years gone by
Some bringing a chuckle, others moisture to the eye
Like cooking the turkey, the plastic giblet bag inside
Iris and I, inebriated chefs, we laughed till we cried.

Mum wasn't too happy with her knife and fork poised
Cutting through that plastic, made one hell of a noise
But Dad didn't mind, in fact he licked his drooling lips
As we cooked an alternative, his favourite egg and chips!

TURKEY FIGHT

The shops look like the Marie Celeste
With panic buying at its best!
Worse than lockdown, or so they say
Queues are deadlier than Boxing Day!
Grabbing the loo rolls, meat and cheese
Nothing to do with the impending freeze
What's wrong with people, the world's gone mad?
Fighting over Turkeys, so very, very sad
Why not have a street party, share out the spoils?
So everyone has a festive Christmas,
not just The Royals!

TOP OF THE TREE

Christmas wishes warm the room,
The fire crackles in the grate.
The familiar tree twinkles,
The poor old fairy's in a state
It worries her after all this time
That she is always tucked away,
Isolated on the highest branch
Important for just one day!
Tradition says she must stay on top;
It's the most important place to be
And yet, if the tree tumbles over,
She will be the last to climb free.

Lightning Source UK Ltd.
Milton Keynes UK
UKHW010852210622
404740UK00005B/680